2

SHINY AND HER WARDROBE OF VIRTUES

KINDNESS

THE QUALITY OF BEING FRIENDLY, GENEROUS AND CONSIDERATE

BY

Sukanya Shah

BIRCH
BOOKS

First published by Birch Books 2020

ISBN - 978-81-949495-6-5

Email : books.birch@gmail.com

To Adyana.
My first. My all.
May you always be more.

❖

From the Author's Desk

Cossetted in our homes during the thick of the Covid-19 pandemic, I made every effort to keep my toddler happy and engaged. It made me wonder about the true legacy in learning that my child will bequeath. I cannot wait to pass on this treasure of a less than perfect world to her… one that will astonish her most often, teach her most definitely and hold her to two constants—challenge and change.

Shiny And Her Wardrobe Of Virtues was born of this sentiment. Shiny is a spritely little girl who owns a magical wardrobe, with virtuous items that on adorning, change her world view…virtues that go beyond the classroom and make her feel happy and whole.

I enjoyed writing these stories of gratitude, kindness, confidence, patience and love…but more so, I enjoyed diving into these most beautiful emotions and feelings with my child.

I hope you do too.

Love,
Sukanya.

One Friday evening in Virtueville,
The grass was green, the trees were still.

The clouds turned grey, the sun began to set,
Shiny felt a drizzle, the streets were wet.

She swiftly put on her raincoat, with its very own "kindness" hood,
And rode off on her cycle, as fast as she could.

This red raincoat she wore, was of a special make,
It beamed this dreary evening, it made her heart awake.

As she zipped passed to take cover, and escape the heavy rain,
She saw a little pussycat, all wet and mewing in pain.

Crouched under a tree, sat this little cat,
Shivering and scared, she purred “M-m-my n-n-name is Chatte”.

"Oh no!" exclaimed Shiny, "you poor little thing",
Her red raincoat of kindness, shimmered and went abling.

She opened her arms out, and held Chatte tenderly,
Thought teary little Chatte, "this girl is so lovely".

To help someone in need, to understand their fears,
Makes them feel loved, and wipes away their tears.

Off Shiny went, with Chatte in tow,
Riding back home, her raincoat went aglow.

She dried Chatte off, and gave her warm milk,
Then cuddled her warmly, in a blanket made of silk.

To see Chatte finally smile, and purr happily,
Made Shiny's heart swell, with joyful glee.

Kindness is magical, it makes the heart glad,
It spreads joy and love, and takes away what's sad.

FARM
FRIENDS

The next day little Chatte, was dropped off to a farm,
She'd be loved and looked after, she felt thankful and calm.

Chatte was truly grateful, she'd remember this forever,
Shiny's sweet act of love, she'd forget never.

Being kind to everyone, is a lovely way to live.
The magical thing about kindness, is that you get more than you give.

Talking points for parents:

- Ask your child what they understand by kindness?
- Tell your child about an act of kindness you recently did.
- Ask your child how they felt when you were kind to them.
- Maintain a kindness log, with one, simple act of kindness per week – assign a gold star for each act. Four stars allow your child to receive an act of kindness from you.